Merry Christmas
This is a very special
book for a special person.
A book for the ever searching.

Warren & Sadie

I, Monty

Text by Marcus Bach

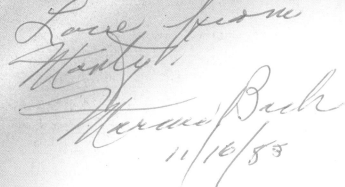

SECOND TRADE EDITION 1980

Published by
Island Heritage Limited
828 Fort Street Mall
Suite 400
Honolulu, Hawaii 96813
Phone: (808) 524-7400

Library of Congress Catalog Number 77-82232
This edition first published in Japan
Printed and bound in Hong Kong under the
direction of Mandarin Publishers Ltd.

Deluxe: ISBN 0-89610-000-6
Trade:　ISBN 0-89610-072-3

Do you suppose
a caterpillar knows,
its future lies
in butterflies?

Chrysalis

Here I was in this lovely grove on a warm and sunny day. I was dangling from a friendly twig, shaded by a large green leaf, thinking how calm and peaceful life could be. All day something had been saying, "Enjoy your world," and this is what I was doing. I was not demanding anything or envying anyone or wanting anything more than just this quiet afternoon with the earth and sky.

Now during this deepest moment, with the
dream of just being me within reach, I discovered
I was weaving layer upon layer of filmy threads
around myself. I was spinning these jade-green
strands covering my legs and body,
slowly wrapping myself
like a mummy in
a shroud.

I used to weave
strands like this in my mind,
but never for real. Often when
I thought about my life, how I
tried to work things out day by day,
comparing myself with others, others who
could fly, let's say, while all I could do was
crawl, I got wrapped up mentally. Those were
strands of my own making. Thought strands.
Now here were real strands wrapping me.

Gradually I   began coiling some around my head and—would you believe it—over my eyes. I could feel the sun through my leafy-green umbrella, but as for light, it was going out. Darker and darker. Yet it all seemed so natural that without being afraid or wanting an answer, I said to myself, "Hey! Can this be dying?"

"Could be, could be," whispered a series of voices and this was amusing because they were my own voice or voices playing tag with each other, chasing each other around and chanting, "Could be, could be," while the truth was it did not matter to me whether my question was answered or not. Either I was still alive or else the dream did not end with dying, so why worry?

Unconscious of breathing, I was conscious of seeing on the screen of my mind the story of my life from the time I first saw the light of day to the present. It was all here, an open book replayed inside the strands that held me in the shroud. It was as though I were in a darkened theater premiering this private showing. But oddly enough as I watched my lifetime spectacular, I was conscious of only three episodes repeating themselves as if they were the peak happenings in my entire story: the meadow, the pavement, and the moment of love.

Out of a total stretch of earthly existence these
three remembrances were rungs in a ladder suspended
in space, a ladder holding me gently while my body,
cased in the shroud, began disintegrating around me.

I was watching myself coming unglued, everything
detaching itself from everything else as if asserting
its own right to live apart from me—eyes, ears, legs,
all going their own way—while I, whatever *I* was,
remained relaxed on the rungs of the ladder, dangling
content on an invisible string, a part of and yet apart
from all that was going on in the shroud.

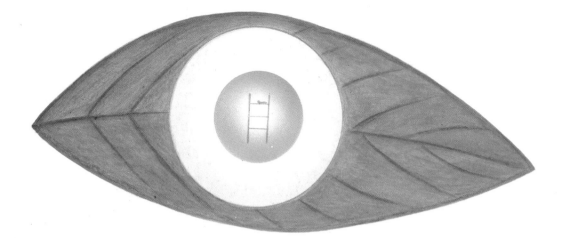

I was a spectator, observing myself, aware of myself, realizing that now with no eyes to see I saw everything. With no body to feel, I felt everything. And instead of being afraid, I sat enchanted on the rungs of the ladder, fascinated by what was going on.

It was as though the grove was suddenly the world and the world was the milkweed patch in the meadow and everything was simply a projection of me.

That eye, for example, the eye down there in the shroud, the eye that had once been mine, what a marvelous thing it was, able to get along by itself! Hadn't there been two eyes? No matter. The eye I was seeing was all light, a silver spear of light prowling inside the shroud. It was an eye-at-large, you might say, an all-seeing eye.

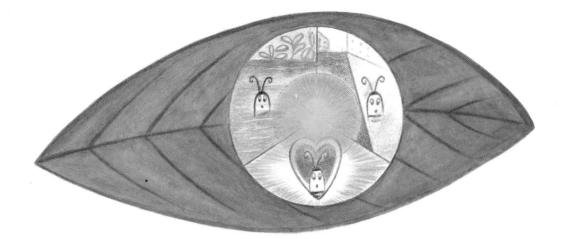

"If this was my eye," I told myself, "and it is down there lighting things up, then with what kind of an eye am I seeing?" Who has ever seen his own eye? All I ever saw was the reflection of my eyes, as when I looked into a pool of water one day in the meadow, or saw myself in the shimmer of the hot pavement, or when I looked into her eyes in that moment of love. "How," I wondered, "can the eye see the eye unless it is a universal eye? Is that the way I am seeing things now?"

"Could be, could be," said my voices, and at this, the scene burst into rainbows of colors. Inside the shroud a shower of cosmic colors erupted, colors galore flashing out in interlacing rings, blending and merging as if a master decorator were riffling through chart after chart for his prime customer, turning the pages as if life always had a choice, and saying, "Take your pick, you there on the ladder, and take your time. We have all the time in the world."

Now the parts of my body that had been going their separate ways were reunited by an inner attraction. Then they began to dissolve, merging into each other with wavelike motions, then settling into a shapeless mass that pushed against the inside of the shroud in a dead weight.

A dead weight. That was my cue. Sure as you're born, I *was* dying. I was on my three-runged ladder, swinging, an enchanted watcher over my demise, never once doubting that this was part of the dream.

Not that I didn't feel a personal involvement. Heaven knows I did, but it all conformed so closely to what I had always imagined dying would be like, that it more than complemented my expectations.

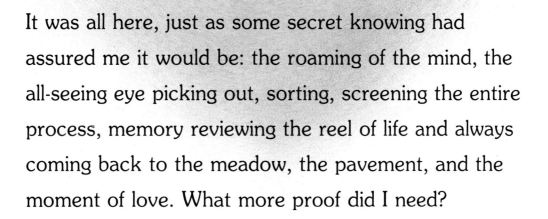

It was all here, just as some secret knowing had assured me it would be: the roaming of the mind, the all-seeing eye picking out, sorting, screening the entire process, memory reviewing the reel of life and always coming back to the meadow, the pavement, and the moment of love. What more proof did I need?

"So this is death," I told myself. "At last a new experience."

Then I heard music.

I heard music and had the sensation of the twig being snapped off, I along with it, and carried by an unseen hand. The swinging ladder, I now realized, was the rhythm of a person walking, carrying me carefully but letting me swing, while in his other hand he had a music box of some kind.

This Shadow Man, or whatever he was, had picked me up out of the grove and was carrying not only me, but the shroud. And the shroud was on the twig to which the leaf was still attached, and the ladder and I were held by an invisible connection, as we had been throughout life as far as I was concerned.

It is easiest simply to say that wherever the shroud went in the dark, I went with it in the light, and the light and the dark were one and the same to me. And even though the music was not sad, it sounded like funeral music, happy funeral music, exactly the kind I would have wanted had I known this would happen to me. But who expects this to happen even if he knows it will?

The Shadow Man walked and walked, whistling with the music, swinging my ladder as if glad he had found me and saved me, though just now I had no idea what I was being saved from or for.

Finally he reached a place where he opened a door and laid me on a hard slab. Where this was or what it was I could not say because I could not see. All I saw was the shroud over which I was hovering, but I did have a good sense of feeling.

He laid my shrouded body down. Then he went away, taking the music with him. How lonely that music sounded when it knew it had to leave me! It kept sending back its sounds as if assuring me it did not want to go, but it was carried in stronger hands than mine.

Now I realized that children began filing past the shroud, children whom I could suddenly see but who apparently could not see me. This was understandable. I could not see my real self either, but I always knew my body was there and I knew that the dead weight in the shroud was part of me, and I knew now that those threads and strands were really not of my own making. They were part of the dream.

The children looked at the shroud and glanced at one another as if imagining themselves wrapped inside those strands, as if wondering how it would feel or if there was any feeling. A freckle-faced boy planted his hands on his hips and said, "Hmm, isn't that something!" Then a sandy-haired youngster slyly nudged the shroud and said, "He's dead." Another boy thrust out his hand and also touched the shroud. "Yep," he said, "he's dead all right."

A pretty blue-eyed girl whispered, "It's not nice to touch dead things. Is it, teacher?"

Sure enough, there was a teacher sitting thoughtful and smiling in the center of the group. She must have been there all the time, but I did not see her until the blue-eyed girl referred to her.

Could it be, I wondered, that the dead see the living only when they are mentioned, and was it possible that the living only see the dead this way too?

At any rate, when I saw the teacher I had the sensation that she saw me. I was supposed to be invisible on my swinging ladder, but I know she saw me because she smiled and nodded with a faraway look in her eyes.

A quiet boy, sun-tanned, with long black hair, turned to the teacher and said, "He's not really dead. Didn't I find him in my father's grove and bring him here and lay him on the desk? Didn't I carry him gently, whistling all the way?"

"You may think you carried me," I said to myself, "but it wasn't really you. It was the Shadow Man."

But if the boy wanted to believe he found me and carried me, well and good. Let him have *his* dreams. I was sure the teacher knew about these things because she put an arm around the long-haired boy and said, "Maybe being dead is not what we think it is."

"Maybe it isn't,"
I felt like saying, because
here I was on my three-runged
ladder, here I was asleep in the
shroud, and here I was a memory
in the meadow where thousands
like me were still crawling,
grubbing for food,

working for a right to live, wanting to be noticed yet not
wanting to be seen, each one staking out his claim in
the milkweed patch and trying to make himself secure.

I would not have admitted this to everyone, but truly I had been different than all those others in the meadow. At least, I liked to think so.

"Don't you think I was different, teacher?"

She was sitting at her desk gazing half-smiling at the shroud. She was alone, thoughtfully tapping a tiny golden scale of the kind on which you weigh letters, very light letters. She was tapping this scale when I said, "Don't you think I was different?"

"Of course, you were different," she agreed.

"Thank you," I said. "I don't mean that I didn't try to get the best and biggest milkweed pads in the meadow or that I was above frisking a leaf or two from a luckier neighbor. That was part of the game. If I hadn't taken them, others would have. Wouldn't they? But something inside me was different. Others would never have understood me if I had shared my deepest feelings with them. You know?"

"I know," whispered the teacher, as if everyone who had ever talked to her from his swinging ladder had told her the same thing.

"Has anyone ever figured out," I asked, "why some must work in the milkweed patch and others own the patches? Could you tell me, please, why there are times when the biggest, juiciest leaves are just within reach until we reach for them and then they slip out of reach? Who or what regulates these things? What kind of a game is it? And who can tell me why I feel so good on my swinging ladder even when I don't have the answers, and why is it that even though the dream is always beyond us we never lose the dream?"

She looked at me, looked through me, I might almost say, and then laughed softly to herself.

After a while she said, "What about the pavement?"

"You know how pavements are," I said. "Crowded. Hot. Cold. Dusty. Wet. Slippery. You can be crushed to death on the pavement. You must really fight for your life on the pavement. That's another thing. Why is it that some can fly above the pavement and others have to crawl? Have you ever thought about that, teacher, and do you think that's fair?"

She nodded thoughtfully as if weighing what I had said on her golden scale.

Why, I wondered, didn't she ask me about the moment of love. Why didn't she ask me about that?

She didn't, but then I realized that the children
had returned. I caught sight of them all at once,
sitting at their desks, eyes fastened on the teacher,
eager eyes staring, globs of eyes watching and
listening as if they, too, were asking the questions
I had asked and waiting, as I was, for answers. But

they could not see me. All they could see was the
shroud. I, at least, had seen inside the shroud and
I remembered the colors and the flames and the
various parts of me having a life of their own while
I observed it all from my swinging ladder. And I
remember how I had been found and saved and how
the music and the dream were with me all the way.

Slowly the ladder stopped swinging as if warning of the ultimate plunge into wherever the dream was leading me.

"Good-by, world," I whispered. "Good-by, meadow. Good-by, pavement. Good-by, children," while I wished with all my heart I could try it all over again. The thing called life had been all too brief. Sometimes seemingly endless moments, now a quick and sudden end. If I had only known earlier the little more that I knew now!

"Teacher? Can you hear me, teacher? Are you there?"

No teacher. No children. No one to whom I could talk to about the longing in my heart.

That had always been the worst of things, to feel I was trusting in something or someone who might not be trusting in me. Something or someone had set the whole thing in motion, given us the dream and then run off to hide, and we were all either trying to find him or hide, too, or work things out somehow without knowing whom to trust and never quite reaching our highest or living our best or believing that anyone could ever understand. "That's sad," I told myself, "that's really sad, but would you do it differently if you could do it all over again?"

"You see," I found myself saying to myself, "we were all so busy with those milkweed leaves in the meadow and so tired on the pavement. So tired. So many of us, dear teacher, so many. Understand?"

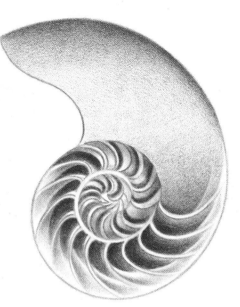

I was not swinging any more. I was suspended in space and instead of falling or rising or having any special sensation, I heard a still, small voice, little more than the catch of a breath, whispering, "Hello, there! What about that moment of love?"

WHAT ABOUT THE MOMENT OF LOVE?

I had that in the back of my mind, but felt it was my jealous guarding of the thought that kept me on the ladder and that if I ever shared that moment with anyone, down I'd go. So I kept it in the dark, so to say, even though it was the lightest, brightest moment in my remembrance.

Now the question and the questioner hovered over me, and I felt that this Shadow Man, whoever he was, would surely understand. So I said, "May I tell you about that moment of love?"

No answer.

"Sir, are you there? May I tell you? It was as though I had wings during that moment. And she had wings. Sir, are you listening? She said to me, 'I am more like myself when I am with you than when I am alone.' And then she said, 'Will you always remember that, Monty?' That was my name, sir. Monty. Do you understand?"

No answer, but my words were enfolded in music and caused a light to rise like a lovely dawning in the shroud, a golden light, silver gold, green gold, pure white gold.

It flashed through my mind that this had all happened before while just as clearly it seemed a foreshadowing of something still to come.

It was like the music and the shroud when I was being carried here. The light and the dark were one. And that is how it seemed with what was going on now in the golden interior of the shroud and what was happening to me on the ladder. The light in the shroud and the light around me as I hung without any visible support were one.

I was alive and dead. I was alone and I was surrounded by presences. I was dying and I was being born. The music was playing and everyone in the meadow was singing and everyone on the pavement was dancing and calling to me, "Hey Monty, what's happened to you?"

I was too happy and too free to answer. I was high, so high they couldn't really see or understand. For once, for one little while, I was living the dream.

I have no idea how long this ecstasy, this interplay between worlds, so to say, went on because the children kept coming and going and saying, "He's dead all right."

"Are you sure he's dead?"

"Everything must die."

"That's the way it is."

"If he's dead why does he move and if he isn't dead why does he lie so quiet, wrapped in his shroud?"

The teacher was patient. Putting her arms around the children, she seemed to be telling them they could never get inside the dream or understand about the silken threads until they went through the experience themselves.

All this time the Shadow Man and the music were there inside the shroud. Sometimes I saw him, then he vanished only to reappear in another place. With the tip of his finger he touched the dead weight in the shroud and it moved. He touched another part and it magically disappeared or it changed color and began to tremble as if it were alive.

This went on for days, seven days to be exact, and then one afternoon when the children filed past the shroud, they stood for a long time gazing at it as if they could finally see through it, enough at least to catch a glimpse of the golden light.

While standing there, one of the smallest of the youngsters shocked the last flicker of life out of me by suddenly thrusting out his hand, giving the shroud a squeeze and shouting, "How you doing in there, Mr. Shadow Man?"

I tried not to hear, but I did. Calling *me* Shadow Man as if I were the weaver of the strands and the light-bearer and the music-maker and the great magician all wrapped in one!

"Am I really? Tell me, sir," I burst out, "are they *all* in *me*?"

There was no answer, but my voice of many voices began to chant around me, "Could be, could be," as if they were anxious to do their part.

A stranger who once met me on the pavement
and with whom I talked about the dream of life
told me that before we die, we catch a quick vision
of life to come. That meeting with him flashed
back to me now, and in this last moment I saw
the beating of wings like pinpoints of color against
the sky and I was whirling in the midst of them.
It was like gazing upward into a lake of liquid light
and if I did have one more breath I must have caught
and held this final one while asking if it truly could
be a preview of things to come.

That was my last remembrance. It was as if a voice within me said, "Come, Monty, it is time."

Before another heartbeat, the darkness, soft and kind and silken, pulled its shrouded curtain down to tuck me in. And that, as far as I was concerned, was the end of me.

Freedom

It was light. I could not remember a lighter, brighter moment and amazingly I was creating the light by working my way out of a jade-green shroud, parting it with wings I never knew I had.

I had been in a dark cell when a voice said, "Come, Monty, it is time," and I responded by twisting and turning as if that would get me out. It didn't. Twisting and turning are not the way. You must find your wings and use them as if you were already free. You are not free, but you have found the way to freedom and the wings are part of the dream. The more you use them the stronger they become and the more the shroud gives way. That is how I got out and found myself hanging steadily to the sturdy rung of my escape ladder which was part of the shroud itself.

My body quickly gained strength. My eyes began to focus. Eyes within eyes. As far as I was concerned, I was being born with the excited feeling of having come through an endlessly long night, a night with no remembrance excepting silence and the dark.

Yet
I must have
brought some
memory with me
out of the past be-
cause as I balanced
myself on my one-runged
ladder dangling from the
shattered shroud, I saw a
group of children's faces and had
the feeling I had seen them before.
Then as my vision cleared I saw a
kindly, smiling woman and I knew she was
a teacher even before one of the youngsters
whispered, "What's his name, teacher?"

Before she could answer, a freckle-faced
boy spoke up, "Don't you know? It's Monty!"

The word sent a thrill through me and I turned my eyes on him. He was right. I was Monty.

My name was whispered among the children and they said, "How are you, Monty? You're beautiful. You're neat. We love you. Hi, Monty."

They wanted to touch me, but something held them back.

"It's Monty," the teacher reassured, putting her arm around a blue-eyed girl while looking steadily at me.

My world grew lighter and brighter. I felt close to this group but something told me to keep my distance. On the one hand I wanted to be happy and trusting, anxious to try my wings, but I also wanted to close in on myself protectively in a world that was becoming breathlessly exciting. I had come into it so mysteriously, bringing so much of the past and yet no memory of it, so much of hope and expectation, yet no actual proof that things would be as I hoped, and while I could hardly wait to fly, I clung to my ladder in thought. Where had I come from? Why was I here?

A quiet boy deeply tanned, long-black hair, looked at me as if reading my mind. Turning to the teacher he said, "Does Monty know who he is?"

"I don't think so," replied the teacher.

"Does he know where he came from?" the boy asked. "Does he know I carried him here from my father's grove? Does he remember the music?"

The teacher shook her head. "They never do. Well, hardly ever."

"Then they're not very smart," a chubby boy spoke up.

"Monty's smart," protested the blue-eyed girl.

"Monty's different," said the long-haired boy, almost to himself. "Aren't you different, Monty?"

I groped back into the dreamless night. Something came through but nothing was clear, so I stayed on the ladder until the children and the teacher went away. I could tell by the warmth coming through the window that it was late afternoon. I could see by the trees in the school-yard that it was autumn. The classroom was very still. I decided to leave the ladder and take off.

What gave me the courage? You don't just let go of a ladder, you know.

Nor would I have let go but for the music. There was this happy kind of birthday music all around me. The room was singing, something inside me was saying, "Let go, Monty, let go!"

I took a deep breath. I let go and something lifted me as if I had been practicing this all my life, as if I had been born with this very thing in mind.

What an experience! Lifted and guided, I was effortlessly transported to the light. I was at the window, free as a feather, looking out, wondering whether it was the music that carried me or whether I carried the music.

The question was answered almost at once. As I rested on the window sill, the shadow of a large impressive figure moved back and forth outside the window as if he controlled the world.

The trees and the sky and the out-of-doors were clear and beautiful, but by a slight change in focusing my vision, so that I could look deeper into things, I realized that this Shadow Man kept moving continually through all of nature and nature moved through him. You could say, "The world is wonderfully clear," and that was true, but as you looked closer you realized he was there in everything, and the more he was there the clearer things were, as though he wasn't there.

As I thought about this, he suddenly came through the closed window as if *it* wasn't there. The faces of the children were mirrored in him as was the face of the teacher and I

could see how happy they were. Of course, they were not really there, they were merely reflected in him and that may have been the case with everything, nature, the classroom, and even me. All may merely have been reflections.

At any rate this Shadow Man came in and moved about the room as if he owned the place, then paused and noticed me. Looking me over he said, "Well, Monty, you turned out quite all right."

I zigzagged around the room in a happy sort of dance, finally lowering myself to a golden scale on the teacher's desk, a bright, shining scale that seemed to have been placed there just for me.

This was where the teacher found me on the following day. She found me on the scale and said, "Good morning, Monty," while the children gathered around and said, "Hi, Monty, how did you sleep? What do you want for breakfast?"

"Cabbage," said a boy.

A girl laughed. "Cabbage! He doesn't eat cabbage."

"He doesn't eat anything," the blue-eyed girl spoke up. "He drinks."

Then she and the teacher and the long-haired boy showed them what I had been drinking out of a shallow bowl covered with a bit of gauze that let a mixture of honey and water filter through.

"What's that?" the children asked.

"Nectar," said the blue-eyed girl. "You see he doesn't eat cabbage. He never heard of cabbage. Did you, Monty?"

How could I have heard of it since I had just been born?

Whenever I wanted to travel around the room I simply tuned in to the music and something lifted me. It was a most wonderful arrangement and I was happy about the whole thing until I made a startling discovery: I was free but I was still a captive. I was out of the shroud, but the classroom was just as confining.

The Shadow Man with the music could come and go as he wished. Walls and windows meant nothing to him. But had you seen those windows you would have felt as I did. You couldn't open them by yourself and you couldn't break them without hurting yourself, and you couldn't wish them away.

As for the teacher and the children, whenever they left they locked things up tight. As far as I was concerned the classroom was another shroud. So every

night when the Shadow Man came with the music and poked around inspecting his world and checking on the records of the children, I said, "Please, sir, show me how to go through solid things the way you do."

One night, as if weary of having me plead with him, he said off-handedly, "You know how to get out. The trouble is you do not know that you know. You know what lifted you, don't you?"

"The music, sir?" I asked.

No answer.

"Wings?"

Silence.

"Love, sir?" I ventured.

"Whatever lifted you," he said impatiently, "will set you free."

Then he disappeared in the magical way he had of being visible one moment and invisible the next, or of simply letting me form my own opinion whether or not he was there.

I tested the windows and the walls. I tapped the floor and the ceiling and those things were solid. I rested on the scale in thought and just when it seemed that the classroom was a prison with no escape, it dawned on me that there are more ways than one to go through solid things.

One morning, after the usual, "How are you, Monty?" and "We love you, Monty," I stood on my invisible ladder and instead of resenting the children and the teacher for not letting me out, I tried loving them for protecting me and keeping me in. This took a bit of doing but I said, "I love you, too. I don't understand you. I don't know why you wall me in, but I love you. I really do." And I did. In fact, I went to each one of them and touched them with my wings to prove I meant what I said.

At this, they gathered around the teacher and began talking excitedly, clapping their hands while some actually looked sad as they glanced my way. Whatever they had in mind was special, for when the teacher nodded as if to say the time had come, there was a long silence during which they looked at me with a love I could trust and which I truly wanted to return.

The tanned, long-haired boy walked to the window. With a flip of his hand he unlocked it and opened it wide and high. I will never forget that moment, the way he turned to me as if to say, "You wanted to go through solid things. Okay, Monty, go on." There were tears in his eyes and his voice trembled, but he looked at me manfully and said again, "Go, Monty, here's your chance."

The children lined up at the window. They formed two lines with space between for me to pass. The air from the outside came into the room fresh and fragrant. It echoed the thoughts of the boy, "Okay, Monty. You wanted to get out of the classroom. Go on."

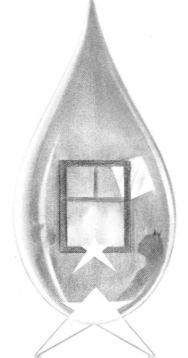

I want to go, but now that I can, I want
to stay. Something draws me and something holds me,
and for once I wish someone would make the decision
for me and let it go at that.

"Why doesn't he go?"

"He's afraid."

"He's not afraid."

"I'll make him go!"

"He'll go by himself," the teacher said.

She was right. Even though my feelings were opposed, something told me to let go and be lifted as I had been so many times before.

So I did. I let go, and in no time at all I was on the other side of solid things as if they had never been there.

That was something to remember, a moment filled
with music of a kind that told me the Shadow Man
had pulled out all the stops, while the children pressed
against each other, leaned out of the window, waved
and clapped their hands and called, "'Bye, Monty!
Happy landings! We love you, Monty!"

But the long-haired boy stood alone, crying. And
I saw the blue-eyed girl go over and put her hand in his
while the teacher stood smiling as if she had lived through
this same scene in this same way when she was young.

While I did a little dance for them outside the window, something drew me as if I were on a string, drew me into the open windows of the world which no one can close, and the next thing I knew I was sipping nectar from a ruby red rose on my first full day of freedom. In something louder than words I heard myself say, "Thank you, teacher! Thank you, Shadow Man. You were with me before I ever got my wings."

In that moment it all came back to me: the grove, the strands, the shroud, the colors and the golden light. Framed into that recall was the vivid memory of the meadow, the pavement, and the moment of love, and I realized that what I had thought was death and dying was actually being born. What I had considered darkness was that which had to be, and I knew with all my heart that this had happened to me over and over since time began, and not to me only, but to everyone.

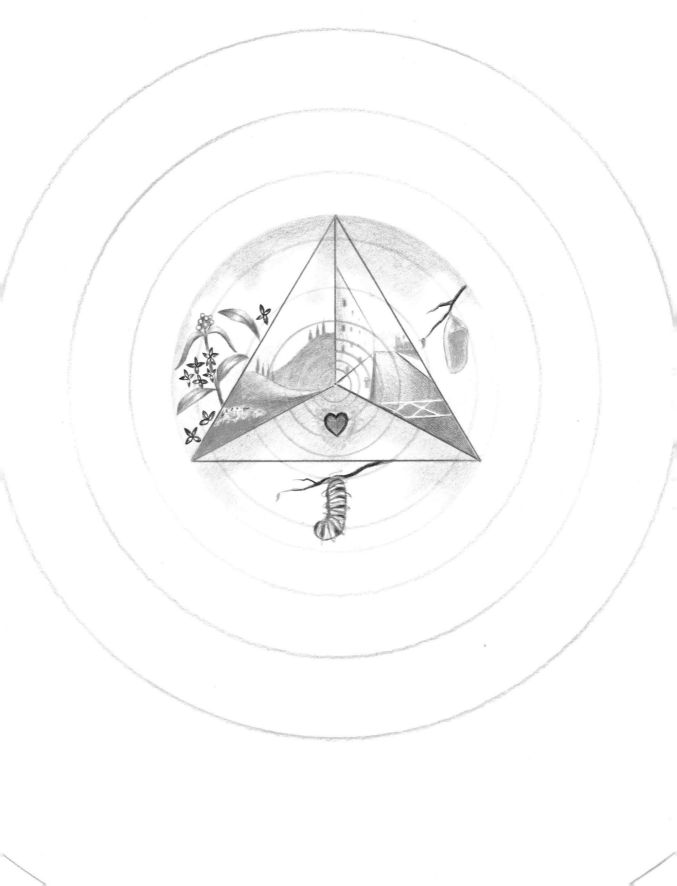

I dance from flower to flower, filling my lungs with fragrance and my body with the intoxicating spell of nectar, not quite knowing why I am doing what I do until I feel the warm touch of pollen on my wings, I see it rub off of one flower and rub on to another and I know there is meaning in my life though no one else might believe it or see it or understand. I go from place to place and scene to scene, telling myself that but for me the flowers would die and the world would fade and even the Shadow Man and the teacher would have a hard time keeping the earth lovely and alive—were it not for me. That is how important I am in my life and time.

So I began to travel. Flower to flower, garden to garden, tree to tree, waking, sleeping, travel and rest, travel and rest in a world that has me guessing every moment of the way whether it made me or whether I am making it as I go along.

There are days so beautiful and kind I am sorry to see them end. I dream about them in my sleep. There are days when the wind tears at me and the rain drives me to the ground. Days when sand gets on my wings, the dense air chokes me, the cold stabs me, I am frightened and fly as hard and as fast as I can to hide myself or find a place to camouflage my fears. I ask myself: do I run away because I am afraid, or am I afraid because I run away? Am I sad because I cry or do I cry because I am sad? Which comes first and who or what am I controlling or who or what is controlling me? I believe in the Shadow Man, but does he believe in me? If I trust him will he trust me? Who should first prove his trust?

Then I remember the classroom and how I learned to go through solid things and how the window was opened by the long-haired boy standing there looking out over the world, how the flowers were ready and waiting and how the voice said, "You turned out quite all right."

When these things got through to me I realized that even when life was not right, it was right, and when I imagined I was in the wrong place it was not wrong and whatever was happening was as it was supposed to be.

One morning I heard the flutter of a flock of whirlwind wings other than my own. My flight was southwestward as it had been ever since I left the classroom. I had usually been alone. Now waves of golden wings stirred the sky, enfolding me in a galaxy of motion. Whether I joined them or they joined me is not clear. I only know that on this magic morning when the season changed, I felt myself multiplied a million times, a million Montys crossing the mountains and catching sight of the open sea.

The full wonder of the Shadow Man burst over me. To think that he could have made so many others exactly like me and yet no two alike. If someone had picked me out of the maze and said, "Run scared," or if someone had caught me now, crushed me, stabbed me, shot, poisoned, choked or drowned me, I would still have been me because everyone was me and I was everyone.

It was like the music moving through us. No one could possibly have destroyed that. How would we have traveled without it? What would have steered us? Just as I asked myself again what would have lifted me had it not been love?

Love brought me into the millions like myself
and when we found ourselves among the towering
eucalyptus groves above a little village near the
sea, love held us there. Love was reciprocal. When
we descended wing to wing, casting cloudlike
shadows on the ground, people looked up, cheering
and clapping their hands.

At first the shrubs and gardens called us.
Then we were drawn upward to the dangling moss
on oaks and cypress, finally swarming to the jewel
trees with their spikes of golden-yellow blossoms.
Here we rested, blended into nature.

There were days when great crowds of people
walked and talked among us thoughtfully. Children
and teachers, young and old, parades and floats,
music and singing, no mourners now, no shrouds,
no darkness. All was love and light.

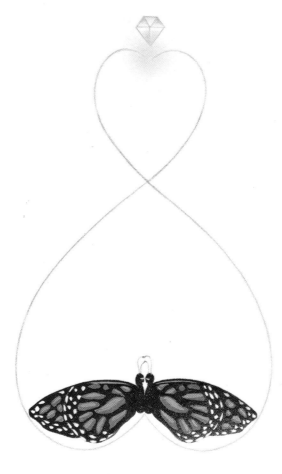

If love brought me into the millions like myself, the same love made me leave them on an appointed day to find my own true love. That is how it was. There came a time of special need for someone to love in the midst of loving and being loved, someone both alike and different from those who were copies of myself.

The quest began with a response to
the music, the feeling of letting go
and being lifted, a sudden pull on
all the senses and something
saying, "Okay, Monty, it
is time. Come along!"

It was like leaving
the classroom. I
carried the longing
of others with me as
if fulfillment for me
would be fulfillment for
them. It was the same response,
more selfless now and more believable.

I flew between earth and sky, guided by
sensations, cradled in music, drawn toward a sea-green
field where a winding lane was a free, safe path with
milkweed banks on either side. When I saw this, it was
as if something said, "All for you, Monty, all for you."

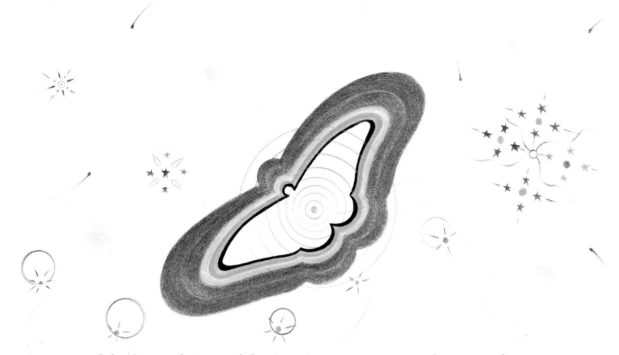

I believed it and knew it was meant for another, too, another solitary other me, guided as I was, by waves of feeling and a secret scent trailing in the sky. I fanned my wings with furious strength, realizing they were filled with power greater than my own. A soft wind distilled the stream of fragrance and stirred the perfume of the milkweed fields. The world seemed safe and free and all this world was mine. I caught the drunken force of it without so much as pausing in my flight. My incredible wings caught the beat of what I was sure were angel voices humming, since words could not express the wonder or the measure of it all.

I am in flight and I am motionless in space. I see her in a flash of silver wings as we greet each other with a secret signal that no one has ever revealed. When you think of it, the universe, I mean, being as vast and immeasurable as it is, it is a miracle that we should find each other, but it would be a greater marvel if we missed each other, chosen as we were to answer the same call, drawn nearer and nearer, fires of gold and green flashing, while the music grows and the chorus of voices rises, and we sense the touch of our bodies in the sky. I could not have let her go, or she me, even if the Shadow Man had wanted us to part. There are laws of love to which he himself is bound.

The voices and the singing drift away until we
are alone. I am on a ladder swinging. I am one with
this someone like myself and she is saying, "Remember,
Monty, how I once told you, 'I am more like myself
when I am with you than when I am alone'?" And the
children are saying, "Of course, Monty remembers!"

I hold my breath for fear this moment of reality
will pass. I see myself again not only in the meadow
and on the pavement, but in this moment of love and
now I know the full meaning of the grove and the shroud.
I feel the cold slab when the Shadow Man in the role
of the long-haired boy laid me on teacher's desk. I
recall the colors and the Chrysalis in the classroom and
I see the commonly unseen in the golden scale and the
open window. I remember being reborn out of what I
thought was death and I break the spell by crying out,
"Why don't you tell everyone how it really is!"

"They know, Monty, they know!" a voice assures me.

Whose voice? It could have been the Shadow Man's or the teacher's or the children's or the voice of her whose body is close to mine. It may have been my own. But though I do not know whose voice it is, I believe it and I get a firmer grasp on life than ever before. It is a feeling and a knowing in the light of the unknown, but to hold to the feeling and to believe that what you feel believes in you, that makes all the difference in the world.

We are borne close
to the earth. I see
the workers in the
meadows and the
tired travelers on
the pavement.
I try to attract
their attention.
I do a dance to
get them to notice
me while my other
self withdraws her body
from mine and together we try to
catch their eyes. They will not look up. We hover
over them. We touch them. They are too occupied.
They shake us off as if envying us our wings.
They do not know that we were once where they
are and they shall be where we are now and that
these transformations are the links and balances
in the chains of time.

I remember long ago, in the mysterious period in the shroud when I was on my three-runged ladder, some did look up and say, "We knew it, Monty, we knew it all the time!" So they must know deep within their toiling and their travel, they must remember, but perhaps, as in my case, they cannot quite believe that it is easy and beautiful if only one can catch the feeling of the total plan.

We are carried back to the open lane. The same wings that carry her carry me. That is how it has always been, the wings are the music and the music is love, and it brings us, as it does everyone, to the green banks and the milkweed fields, and there we rest. That is, I rest on the soft grass and try, as I so often have, to decide what is real and what is merely dreaming. There is no separating the two.

I look up and see her there above me, beautiful, golden, going her own way as if it were my way, going from leaf to leaf in the milkweed field and wherever her body touches a milkweed pad, she leaves a fragile, shimmering, blue-green pearl of life, smaller than a drop of dew.

I lie there in the grass and watch her until she is out of sight, until in fact she disappears as mysteriously as she came to me. I lie there fascinated by her trail of tiny jewels and I concentrate on one so infinitely small it hypnotizes me. I see it move and grow, a speck of light expanding, taking on a halo of milky-white.

Gradually it becomes transparent and I see a movement of life trembling inside. A most remarkable thing. The stirring life has a greenish wingless form and many legs, as I once had. I watch entranced and realize that though I am lying there in the grass, wings quietly together, motionless, unmoving, eyes closed, silent, embracing the earth, I am also already moving in the pinpoint of life.

I do not expect anyone to understand this, even if it has been experienced, I mean my lying there like a pendant while at the same time I am the instar inside the speck of dew, alive, encompassed by a radiant light.

For a moment I am puzzled by the incongruity. Then I catch sight of the Shadow Man. I know Him now. I see Him moving through the world and watch Him come and go through solid things as easily as I went through the open window in my first free flight. In this moment of recognition I am returned to my body and feel myself stirring in the warm and friendly grass. I am one with Him and with all I have ever known. I try my wings and am lifted up. I flutter as on an invisible ladder. I am part of and apart from all this interplay. I am high in the sky in happy flight and I am quietly waiting in the beauty of the earth until I return again.

Music and singing rise everywhere around me
and as I lose myself in the wonder of the sights
and sounds, I hear someone say . . .

"I love you, Monty. Remember?"